Recovery Community

Recovery Community

Conor Mc Donnell

Mansfield Press

Copyright © Conor Mc Donnell 2020
All Rights Reserved
Printed in Canada

Library and Archives Canada Cataloguing in Publication

Title: Recovery community / Conor Mc Donnell.
Names: Mc Donnell, Conor, 1970- author.
Description: Poems.
Identifiers: Canadiana 20200372254 | ISBN 9781771262606 (softcover)
Classification: LCC PS8625.D7745 R43 2020 | DDC C811/.6—dc23

Cover Image: Alex Andreev, *Light*
Editor: Jim Johnstone
Design: Erica Smith

The publication of *Recovery Community* has been generously supported by the Canada Council for the Arts and the Ontario Arts Council.

Mansfield Press Inc.
25 Mansfield Avenue, Toronto, Ontario, Canada M6J 2A9
Publisher: Denis De Klerck
www.mansfieldpress.net

For *Audrey*
sorry for the nightmares

For *Cillian, Pat & Paddy*
sorry for the kilometres

I am waiting for a terrible sentence to begin

I am waiting for a terrible sentence to begin

I am waiting for permission

I am waiting for the world to empty
his war chest of ammunition

I am waiting for him to be shoved
naked onto the streets
tonguing a solitary gold tooth for Quixotic reassurance

I am waiting for bars to fill with traders
speculating on his future

I am waiting for forest and field to reject him
for canopy and tallest corn to consent to the drones

I am waiting for no respite from silent superveillance

I am waiting for ladders to actualize and stilt-walk away
to loiter across alley-mouths like wooden gangs
all leg and tooth and grin

I am waiting for a rash to rise from the brand on his buttock
waiting for shingles belt to lick his haunch like Sticky-Fingered-Hot-Lip

I am waiting for witches
to ascend from stony riverbeds casting reparation spells

I am waiting for the lesson to dawn
to bubble up in passers-by and flood
through social mediums like body-snatcher plagues

I am waiting for this anger to form
something more than outrage

I am waiving my consent

Recovery Community

7   I am waiting for a terrible sentence to begin

I

15 Qui vincit?
18 //911//9/11//
19 Talisman & Brand
20 We Are Shine
25 L'auteur da fe
26 Forget Galway
28 The Lady Waits
30 Dreams of Deep River
31 Universal Mantra
32 Rebar

II

35 Et mu
36 Study of *A Study for the Nurse in Battleship Potemkin*
37 Let's all of us agree, protection is the key
39 The Scalded Sea
45 Another Death in the Family
46 Lewy-body diary
48 The Lady Vanishes
49 On watching *Elephant* & *Hunger* back to back in a single sitting
51 These media glands
52 Thirty-three rants per minute (33 rpm)

III

57 This is the way
58 Monstros Olympus
61 \<runprogram#^nightwatch^_creationsim\>

62	Come on, undone
64	Universal Mantra
65	Brain prepare to withdraw
67	The Lady Returns
69	I'll be there when you die
71	With the end unfolding around us
72	In the event of an emergency
75	Notes
78	Acknowledgements
79	Thank You
83	About the Author

"…it's how so much of us live so much of our lives"
– Christopher Ware

"I wish I took the blue pill"
– Anon

Qui vincit?

This house could hold more empty seats
but the people who would sit in them were put away long ago.

There is no work here *bring out your dead* no bodies left
to pass the piss-test, close the factory down.

Everything is not what you read, old colic torques to form
new cancer, a different diagnosis to ponder,

collections of atypical things eventually typify something
– backpain, beatings, boredom, parties –

get help any time you want to welcome old pain back.
Fill your gap-year wounds with the tiny holes

you poke in everything else, no chemical solution to your God-
sized problem (even when whispered with a little 'g')

You're young you're cute you got your own teeth
the tank ain't close to half-empty yet, plenty left to hock

from home before you hit the riverbank set up camp & bed down
in the shade of men with beards that crawl

and eyes that never move. He'll take you in and keep you dry
spit-shine your new cancer, help you slip

the lure of fools that every moment is momentous. Let a few months
sidle by, shine illusion warm so you can cake inside

the lullaby of your greatest highs. Want no more than the one thing
he gives, for the one thing you have to give to him,

warmth, your grip on the rung, cos you gotta have faith
if you wanna curse God. Blindfold yourself

get a mystery tattoo let new love put its mark on you, look down,

grass pools red beneath you blotting mis-steps and rotten deeds,
smoothing the urgent rush to breathe. Brace

each time you breach a surface, snap back to memories of not waking
up to or from your first O.D., dusky lips mumbling

'I took nuthin.' Remember, you were not plucked from a fading orbit,
you have the constitution and perseverance

of a rash. You are the flightless moth that eats shed skin, and the shedder
too, you are unstoppable, impenetrable, kevlar

yet prickable like a day-old balloon. What do you say when you travel
so far that no one you know

can hear you? Do you mourn the national breakdown? Rage at federal
fugue? You are no longer soft spoken

now you are roughly spat, panhandled from cavitations and rooted
to riverbanks

a ghoul that staggers through gaps in family photographs never having
taken that first step back. You ask too much of water

we can only get so clean, no nudge or gentle cheat can reverse our cycle now.
We leer into morning exhausted from vigilance to a script

we have long absorbed as canon so know you are no more than meat,
tilt your nose to witness starlings clot like clefs and peck

at the threads of your decisions. Blink respite away like moons repel
satellites, crack the back-ups fitted to flood you

with emptiness that weighs you down to drown on dry land in fluid
expressed from deep within your own chest. I'll be

your gravity your creeping beauty the vine that hugs and dresses you best.
I'll be the first thing people see – a recognition –

blinked away to tears. Let them go blind, where minds go man can follow and no man owns the sky so look up not down

where you prick and bleed ... sleep and let your cancers breathe

//911//9/11//

After a week of bossin' & bitchin' it finally comes my time to sleep / Hello baseball hello weekend here's an extra dip in the deep end / What can it hurt everyone's here the water bottles tip like oil-beaks / Refills transfer under bleachers from backpack bottles / What can it hurt it's hot as hell out people fall asleep in the sun / What can it hurt everyone's drinking drunk or dry / People pass out for bunches of reasons / What can it hurt people got four bars in the park someone'll dial 911 before I'm too far gone / One time I'm dying and I think I see all this stuff I probably didn't see at all my brain put a movie on to hide their faces though I did see the medic go into her bag and pull on a second layer of latex before she even thought about touching me / Silly girl she'll learn I'm a smoker not a popper I got blackened fingers proof I've been licking on Satan's guitar / My own children are hugged up all over me you think I'd hurt my own flesh & blood? / Anyway it's not just me / When ambulances pull up sharp next door / Overdosing neighbour / Truck stalled out in the intersection / Overdosing mailman / Quarterback fast asleep on the infield / Homecoming king propped up at the dairy queen laid out for all the world to see / OTC transaction shuffle to the pharmacy withdrawal emergency / I got a disease my teeth hurt I can't eat / I got money on money on money I owe / Last week Penny gave me a narcan dose in Mickey Dee's / She told them it was an epipen and there must've been shrimp in the fish fillet / As if / Now she's no nurse no more the narcan's all shot out but the other supply still hasn't run dry 'cos we learned to live without seat-belts school books safety nets / I sold everything you can think of one time or another condos insurance used cars pharmaceuticals household appliances jewelry heirlooms wedding gifts rings teeth fillings blood before I got tested plasma afterward / AMEN / I curl up in corners eyes on doors never sold nor robbed nobody never hurt kids that wasn't my own / Worst part of overdose is waking up to the tune of *leave 'im lie and let 'im die* / People you know your whole life live next to you work next to you stealing narcan from walmart packed next to pregnancy tests and kotex sucking every crooked penny up till the first cheque bounces last gram of pride just disappears / Had a bad judgement here and there this lifestyle don't stir in smooth with simple everyday living / This town ain't broke beyond repair just lives in a country dumb to its own grief / You know what they say about grievin' next to every graveyard's a motel if you get down you can always get it on / You feel what you gotta feel when you gotta feel it / Delay it a while there's always another signpost to hell 'case you lose your bearings while we're all busy killing ourselves

Talisman & Brand

The rabbit foot, the monkey's paw

A bolt shot through an eyebrow

A ring snaked through a nose above

a mouth beneath a nipple

The cowboy and his cigarette

Five rings on a swimmer's chest

A bullet on a neck chain

A haircut and a motorcade

A mop-top on a brownstone stoop

A slouch beside a trashcan

A memory

A talisman

The scar beneath the brand

We Are Shine

(*The Shining*, 1980)

The Interview

we are wait
we are have an appointment
we are way to making ends meet
five months peace is just what we need
we are quite the story

Closing Day

we are air feels different here
we are presidents movie-stars royalty all the best people
we are cosy for a family perfect for a child
we are show you the kitchen Wendy
we are getting to the ice-cream
we are eat your breadcrumb-trail we are show you trace of something

One Month Later

we are big-wheel chased by gyroscopes through corridor and kitchen

we are softball smacking smallpox blanket looking over maze

Tuesday, Thursday, Saturday & Monday

we are weather we are forecast we are snowstorm
we are want to finish work
we are in here where you don't come in
not your we / we are not your okay
we are omen exorcist amityville
we are lines and signals down
we are big-wheel in the distance big-wheel close-up
we are covering our eyes we are silent
we are tip-toe we are Mickey in the bad-wolf den
two-fold in the mirror we are not what you see
we are tired we can't sleep we are too much to do
we are wishing we are here
we are making up our promises

Wednesday 2:36

we are playing in hallway we are oracle archer plague
we are Apollo at forbidden door danger screaming in sleep in terrible dream
we are Wendy running seeing our pieces
we are little boy in blue we are gashes at the neck we are you did this
we are go for a walk we are screaming breeze in turbine blades
stabbing us in ear we are one deep at the bar
we are bargaining we are what'll it be we are here's what one by one

we are white man's burden temporarily light good credit nonetheless /
in the market for more

we are bargained we are sold we are settlers we are wagons
we are fall and irreparable harm
we are could be a whole lot better we are nothing we can't handle
we are wisdom we are words
we are goddammit we love the lil' son of a bitch
we are any fucking thing for him
we are that bitch as long as we live will never forgive
we are completely unintentional we are could happen to anyone
we are momentary loss of muscular co-ordination

One minute later

we are feet up on the pillow straddling tv we are looking up African lady
we are impossible we are shut down we are stranded we are frozen
we are blocked we are straining to the heartbeat
we are deathbed grimace reality we are seizing control
we are Jack's white hand on lime-green door we are naked in water
we are grinning like goons we are dribble down our self
we are shaking uncontrollably we are seeing from Miami
we are crossing closing distance we are bloody in our ears
we are touched and we are touching
we are kissed and we are kissing Baba Yaga of the bathtub
we are rotten on the breath
we are in and we are laughing we are waiting
we are here when you will call us
...
we are what about the bruises   we are did it to himself
we are no other explanation
we are the episode he had
we are get out we are not going to let you fuck this up
...
we are tin-cans in the kitchen we are music in dead speaker
we are midnight stars and you
we are good to be back we are orders from the house
we are kind of man who likes to know
we are anything you say we are awful mess that tends to stain
we are most important soiree
we are married we are caretaker we have always been here
we are very great talent being used against the will we are wilful
it's the mother we are correcting her
...
we are coming down the mountain
we are Tony
we are Danny gone away
we are try again later

Thursday 8 a.m.

we are intercontinental
we are calling scatman back

we are all play and no work
we are moral
we are contract
we are principle & ethic
we are not gonna hurt you we are
gimme the bat we are GODDAMN

we are shine floor with back of head
we are what are you doing we
are let me out of
here we are what
never happened we are hurt
real bad
we are dizzy don't
leave we are don't run
through house with knives

4 p.m.

we are passed out in the peanuts
we are business we discussed
we are one more chance
we are no greater pleasure
harshest possible manner
we are good as our word

we are scatman in a snowcat
we are reading in the mirror
we are Danny just got back
we are at the door with Jack
we are sliding out the window
we are come-out come-out wherever you are
we are little pigs let me in

we are blow your house down Wendy
we are chopping we are in

we are cavalry come
we are Danny running Jack limping Wendy whimpering
Scatman calling Jack swinging Danny screaming
we are show ourselves to Wendy we are footprints in the snow
we are floodlights in the storm
we are limping into labyrinth we are beast and boiling rage
we are showing Wendy Wendy sees
we are corpses in the lobby we are blow-jobs in a bear-suit
we are clever boy covering tracks
we are bleeding in the lift-shaft we are axeman enters maze
we are Jack the Giant Killer
we are fi-fo-fum we are not the only one we are howling killer-clown
we are family asunder we are finding wrong way out
we are freezing we are jackfrost
we are waiting to be told we are always to be here we are no sad snowman
we are no sorry
we are shining and Wendy in spring in sun-time we are shine again

L'auteur da fe

(*Vertigo*, 1958)

Accept the role of mannequin to become Madeleine again

You could be blondest of islands, an emerald slipped into blood,
a foreign sweetness on red-green spectrum
hovering over the dead

D'entre les morts l'auto da fé no sense no logic no futile gesture
hints that this sculptor cares for his clay. This is how he sees you.
This is how he wants you. It should not matter to you.

(He trains her rehearses her shows her where to stand & how to move
He is direct, not rude, wills her to breathe but dreads betrayal of sentience,
He moves to re-direct her limbs, pauses to close her eyes)

Where did you go? Did you pass beyond our grasp?
Did you fancy maybe you do not deserve this? (knowing you have to die)

As he measures you to fall again (and again) do you even take any notice?
Any comfort in knowledge – wise to the twist – there's no shedding
the dread of watching sleepwalkers slump toward a window-ledge

        (over and over again)?

No matter,
in spite of light & direction you come to see this for yourself

– it is exactly what it appears to be –

You are supposed to die and it has been staged perfectly

Forget Galway

I am a brittle flower beaten softly

"Something has been feeding on me
These muscles need not be such beef
A tender meat is what is called for

Scarce	scant	Protean
I began a careless quark
the question mark of everything I might become

My brain my spine my marrow (call them Vegas)
My meat my glands my surplus skin (call them Elvis
… Achilles of the Strip)

If, on occasion, Vegas dimmed the lights my skin might slip away
or sleep, while safe at home my cancer lies dormant
drugged behind my ribs, swept beneath my breast

Outside of me it's a fraternity cannibal
I allow feed just enough
to keep him slow and stupid, precisely where I can see him

When something resolves to feed on me I resolve to be less food
Within my clipped economy I bend to such improbable angles
triage to an afterlife is easy to project on me

Do not justify to strangers what I never defended to friends
What began as simple impression eventually grew to take on flesh

I dreamt new songs that composed themselves in front of me
Notes swung from staves assembled to parade at tempos
I could count out like the pills arranged around me

I studied the math of my SSRIs
waited an extra week to fill the coming month's prescription
a bare four weeks in February but enough at the weight I plan to be

I never took the easy way, I wasted away to earn this diagnosis
and these meds, let everybody feed on me
wore tank-tops in winter so anyone could see

Took a boyfriend in town as alibi to never eat at home
One day I'm sure he'll sing of me
struggle not to make this in some way about him instead of me

He'll change my favorite song to Regret from 1963
wonder how *Johnny, don't point that gun at me'*
could keep a woman from wading into the sea

I suppose he was never fully at ease
but there was always less at stake for him
than there ever was for me

I could have said my food was being poisoned
That's why I never ate

And now there's even less of me
scrubbed and tucked into hospital sheets
Morning suns arrive as heated pain behind my eyes

(Call them, Mercury)

How it hurts for you to look
How it hurts for me to be seen

Scarce   Scant   Blind   Silent
An untwisted quark finally stretched
from innocent question to exclamation mark"

The Lady Waits

I am in the eye   I am in an ornate white hotel which is on fire

My grandmother is in the next room

Doomed the fire burns slowly   So slowly people freely come and go

I am in the eye but I cannot see the flames

Smoke hangs thinly but clings to the lights

It is quite gorgeous and I want to photograph it

But first I must get to my room

I am in the eye and there is something I must save

I don't know what I'm looking for   How soon

before the floor collapses?   How long is left to capture this?

I am in the eye but I am plagued by interruptions

Everybody hovers or drifts by in slowest motion The elevators

are tarnished gold like the fittings on listing pleasure ships

I am filled with an anxious delight   I am in the eye

but I cannot see to photograph My life acquires an uneasy calm

as when a baby comes and you are told not to push

an ecstasy held up by pressure and pain

I am in the eye of an emergency & I haven't saved a thing

There are cupids carved in the ceilings

Dreams of Deep River

(*Mulholland Drive*, 2000)

No Hay Banda, Diane

could be some sort of clue
could be I know what you have to do
could be I still wish you'd let me do it

Go with me somewhere – right now –
and we'll bend to the end halfway through

This dream is not a window
– open on desolate outskirts over Sunset Boulevard,
closed to Canadian Cinderella singing her way back home –

                                                and in her dream
she ribbons reason round what she wants instead of what she knows

There's a man out back of this place whose face I never want to see
even if it means I keep this rising dread inside forever

And no release for Diane whose delusion was mostly solid
yet the centre would not set

The final kindness of imitation beheld the haint that failed to save her
and, yes of course, it would have been better if somebody had told her

back home in Deep River, Ontario,
No Hay Banda in Hollywood, Betty,

solamente *Silencio*

Universal Mantra

To everything add one

Rebar

Like reeds
surround
secret lakes

Like
rockets
ready for lighting

Rebar extends
from gaudy villas
in Nayarit, Mexico –
a steely promise
of more to come

Rebar stretches
from half-rebuilt
Haitian hospitals –
skinny arms waving
to welcome the rescue –
a hope for more to come

Like hairs
stand on end

like fingers extend
an answer.

Yes!
This will never end

There is always
more to come.

Et mu

Mu is no cow-song

Mu sits on Ozu's grave
– a symbol
etched on a cube of black granite –
an empty attempt to represent nothing
by making a physical mark.

Mu is microscopic too
Unappreciable
without the right equipment.

Up close, **MU** is micron,
protein receptors
anchored deep in spinal cord

to siphon our endorphins,
sip endogenous rewards.

Mu is easily conquered
by synthetic invaders
(fentanyl, morphine, hydromorphone).

Like Mu, we too swim in toxins
and our siren-song is moot,

the lowing of an impassive herd
consigned to chemical pastures.

Study of *A Study for the Nurse* in Battleship Potemkin

(*Battleship Potemkin*, 1925)

She is not perched on a swing-set
caught in the pause between flying and fleeing
angled above boomerangs tethered
to flags and quilts stitched into her skin.

Though space is marked to suggest a container
she is not a figure getting out of a car
nor Muybridge's Dread Trotting. She is not contained
nor is she chained like a dog whose owner is buried nearby.

She is not one man wrestling two men sleeping.
She is not a nurse screaming in invisible rooms.

She holds hard to the chain that would tip her from
potemkin vistas to unmarked tombs.

Let's all of us agree, protection is the key

(*Double Indemnity*, 1944)

*"My story's filled with words I wish I'd thought of by myself
Tipped to the perfect angle every sentence trips my tongue
There's an ugly boredom inside me but to get this story on its feet
let's all of us agree, protection is the key"*

She charmed the pillars to liquid.
She kissed me and I swallowed an earthquake.

The little voice that lives in my stomach
was shoved off a pier in cement shoes.

She hid her teeth inside my mouth
let me spit her own words out,
bored with skin and drunk on style
our crisis slipped into something a little less comfortable.

Her cigarette – chemical antique – cured my breath
while tenement gums ground on
and earthquakes echoed in my jaw.

Her mohair itched my palate like excited little blades.
Our tryst hung knotted round my neck, gags our consummation.

The hunk of concrete in my gut fought to make its way back up
I wondered if she wondered too –

from dead men's silent footsteps to the good ol' boys in shadow
at the back of secret rooms –

I wondered if I told the truth

'Goodbye, baby ... I never loved you too'

So, leave me to my consequence – a minute's silence on the chair, a match strike in the chamber – for lack of easy sense...

I only wanted to see her again, nothing and nobody else

The Scalded Sea

Mister Gray floated undiscovered in the road

tongue edematous, rough from clotted blood

and licking asphalt.

He fell right where they found him

pelvis separated, ribs un-racked and ringing,

lay unnoticed long enough to reassemble sanity.

Not for the last time memory

would ring this moment and journey home to source.

Not for the first time gusts of grim ideation rose.

His act could be a telling of sorts

One where regret is hereditary

and intent is highly contagious.

Beyond the healing of hip and chest

insistent headaches re-route focus

to his fractured skull,

bone is lifted from frontal lobe to bleed a critical pressure.

A carrier bag untended at the foot of his recovery bed,

so easy to slip it over his head

All he shows is shadow.

He grows less than truthful now,

rehabs, weans from pain meds,

recovers enough to limp along.

For all is preparation now

but other operations first

defiant hips, rebellious displacements.

Anesthesia briefly separates him from rumination

returns him to prior spontaneity, older animation

as if the gas stands soluble guard

on the banks of duelling personalities.

When he checks out AMA

he heads for the nearest ferry,

spends an afternoon texting family

acceptable ways to do this thing.

He wanders home, redons old clothes,

for all is preparation now.

He constantly eyes water –

rivers streams pools and puddles –

knowing she can see.

Dropping madness into her heart

he leaves little notes like depth charges

They lead with goodbye, degenerate

to how and why before – disappearing

for hours, ignoring texts and messages –

he returns home disheveled and dry.

Their friends begin to tire.

Gone are challenge & intervention

shifts of appeal from why to *why water*.

Return he'd say, relieved to explain,

and *step away from shadow*.

He tells the story the same every time

no detail displaced

each moment ambered in place.

How he came to

on a roadside in fender and glass

determined to die

while others were tended to first.

He tells the story so many times

his audience becomes the device

through which he becomes the story.

His will exhausts all witnesses

leaving him free to slip unnoticed.

Our own retellings are gradual turning

of backs to land so we might

face uncertain waters.

If not, there is no magic

no wings at our ears

no gills to kiss us goodnight.

We learn to be the driver

appreciate when to brake

reverse and turn around

pull our own selves up and out.

In the end

a night like any other

A film with the kids

A late walk home

Kiss everyone goodnight

and goodbye.

He leaves no note

no regret generator

no easy explanation why.

His story proceeds silently.

He leaves the house

no texts no envelope

propped upon the table.

He boards the island ferry

slips away unseen.

A drowning, a cleansing,

all he showed was shadow before

but clarity, even now, in open water

is doused and held down

by stones in pockets

Another Death in the Family

(*Night of the Hunter*, 1951)

"You gotta play mothers, otherwise you won't have a long career in Hollywood"

Rest a while (just drift), after all we're not going anywhere and every game has its rules. We look out for ourselves when the new guy comes around to better see this fix she's in. We watch her struggle and sink 'cos she's a real left-winger who went down south held possums in her arms but let her chin drop too far down. She holds that smell of something wonderful—a widow with a wad of bills—we watch him woo her marry mama plot against his bride: the killer needs his victim, the hunter needs us blind. But he can't kill the world and she can't bear to hug us all so instead they tell us stories that make us cry until we grow wary of this business she's in for she stands in the way of what men want and think, and this direction will rule or ruin her. Already we recognize dangerous raptures where death is never an accident; the forest harbours us children while the river holds our mothers down.

Lewy-body diary

I thought I was at an earlier stage but it turns out I am not

This is the end of any privacy afforded to my faculties

With increasing acuteness everything counts now

Cracks in things are promise of light, false

I carried on as if I could be capable of

this relentless seam of adjustments

accumulated deletions of ability

consequences of pressing hard

accretion of irrevocable truth

subsidiary shame category

conceal what can be done

begin making concession

intrusive dominant states

accumulated indignities

my world grown small

awaken and inventory

cognitive exfoliation

coercive distraction

nothing hopeful

that's gone too

Bless children

& their future

allow belief

Imagine a

journey I

can still

take &

leave

time

for

us

4

u

i

.

(For Peter R & family)

The Lady Vanishes

On watching *Elephant* & *Hunger* back to back in a single sitting

I am watching Jesus die

        Fassbender fade

and my *Hunger* is all
six-packs and cock

a cachectic vigil
of wounds anointed
and crosses swapped for crowns

I am watching Sands shift through
community and committee to command
disciple and discipline to disband
tourist and turmoil to terrorist
and all I can do is nothing

not bite
not chew
not fight

This torture has a soundtrack
the rhythmic thwack of SWAT batons
on handheld Perspex shields

and I am left to the silence
that follows justice on the fly

…

My *Elephant* is all barrel and bullet
a silent scrum of murder and beauty
on empty featureless streets

The camera points & shoots
shoulder to shoulder with assassins

– those troubadours in 'troubled-times' –
all serious haircuts & shiny shoes
in shitty Nissans & Ford Cortinas

To every death an attendant

To every branch in Eden
a limb from which to swing

But hot knuckles
don't cool quickly
and soldiers scrubbed
raw with religion
take
no prisoners

They make
no communion

These media glands

A new-breed of soldier coughs tumors into their hand behind enemy lines

Drops them into the water supply on pay-per-view before they die

A clockwork surgeon dissects electrical sheep on a digital beach

A 50-foot smile made of donated teeth restores some faith in community

A glint in the eye of the weather-girl is either strong command of crowd

or retina-cams uplinked from smart-TVs to network broadcast

The soundtrack to a ring snaking through a lip wrapped round a nipple

is breaking every online record since online records began

These media glands are talismen buried under brands

Dropped into our water source live-streamed on-demand

Thirty-three rants per minute (33 rpm)

As if we are not Violator
As if we were born just to stand
As if no one saw a darkness
As if the pink robots ever stood a chance

As if the bible is not neon enough
As if the queen was anything but dead
As if a nation dreams at night
As if rust really sleeps

As if the ritual was ever not habitual
As if the fables needed us to reconstruct them
As if the dreams of Siam are not infinitely happy
As if all previous lives were not equally rubbish too

As if people are not automatic
As if music has no right to children
As if you are ever feeling anything but sinister
As if it was not a shame about Ray

As if there's not always a riot goin' on
As if the gilded palaces aren't sin
As if your head is truly not checked
As if we are, any of us, anything but men

As if anyone's fantasy is anything but beautiful dark and twisted
As if caterpillars cannot pimp too
As if nothing could turn itself right-way round
As if the woman would sell the world

As if anyone else could remember it in you
As if bridges ever straddle settled waters
As if the mountain is able to hear us
As if the moon has a bright side at all

As if the first born had lived
As if Heaven's antenna could receive our skinny fists
As if none us are not always floating in space
As if the mantra is non-universal
As if I'd come back in anything but black

III

This is the way

The words not spoken will keep us silent

forge language in stasis to shape our concerns

Our mouths will transplant lights for voices

to nourish and shower the newborns down

The fresh graft will smile back at us

Monstros Olympus

This is money this is taxes

southern accents on CBC

This is morning mist accosting parkland

this is 4 a.m. an hour early

this is perspiration-drip from the tip of a spartan nose

this is boardwalk this is sunrise this is spotify

shuffling through inspiration to fuel exhausted gods

and this

is a pause

This is sparring this is pre-text

this is nike vs cross-fit

this is Jordan catching air

this is monochrome slo-mo of indoor downpour

bulging calves in tightest close-up

pan and zoom and tilt

and this is fade

This is pre-shaving

this is post-juicing

this is Carl Lewis

this is Reagan

this is Ben Johnson

this is victory

This is cuckoo clocks on bedside tables

alarm clocks in the trash

this is death from diabetes

lipoproteins in freefall

this is sex-talk during hiccups

this is abdomen without bone

this is dying in your sleep

this is never taking a punch to the teeth

this is knowledge

this is meat

This is memory of the cave

this is branding this is seeping

this is buried in the tick

this is invisible-ink italics weaved through warrior tattoos

This is recoil of acceptance

this is breaking-in the jaw

this is bicep of a motion

this is seated hyperflexion

This

is just a shopping list

 – uninspired and ugly –

all of us, finally,

coming in first

<runprogram#^nightwatch^_creationsim>

All night, bloated nematode, you slept in my throat
By virtue of hemispheric dreams I could not rear or stand

You grounded me to search for cloth in other trees
rendered dark invisible through gentle cheats of fleshing

Branches – chewed to nibs and dipped in sap –
grind mad-stone pellets into furrowed calcule-grains

Vigilance-rich gumbo-cud plugs drone-pilots into sim-drills
decreasing delays over terminals in dim suburban basements

Come on, undone

dissolve unbidden progeny to rotten luck with chemistry

beat out a rhythm   stir the city   leak onto morning streets

scratch the low-tide watermark of rising spite beneath the debris

not for the weak the heel of the city runs hard and over-exposed

under a bridge a penis fatter in hand than fun-sized soda cans

construction engines crane their necks toward the city's throat

overturned wheelchairs on streetcar-tracks bring commutes to a halt

lose the useless filters   let teeth be the weapons they were made to be

rent a flophouse-room for an hour   fuck for seven minutes   scream

for fifty-three   knock knock who's there dancing on the nightstand

slapping snapping fingers away   can't hear the crystal music

in her inner ear or the turbulence of deep-fried blood

hips don't slap   nails don't crack when hands are clapped

eyes don't bleed from sneezing   help her sit in soothing light

search for bugs she swears are there return some trust in skin

All these deaths feel wrong a taste of cancer on falling snow

a touch of call us when they're done

Universal Mantra

Pause
to sleep

for no better reason than following water to source is exhausting
It will remain until you return

On waking, add one to everything

Search
every heart for a beating god
a throbbing glove
a pulsating womb
every heart for a beating god concealed within a heart

Find
acceptable balance with human thoughts
Stroll alone through Bethlehem at seven minutes to midnight

Dress
all trace of branch & leaf
the angel atop becomes
demi-god of invisible mountains

Stimulate
that part of the brain that maintains inner gravity
Watch yourself float away on repeat
Now is the perfect time to breathe

Return
to source
to solace in wisdom

Prepare
to step aside for children

To everything but us
To everything but us add one

Brain prepare to withdraw

He re-appears
where He first emerged
like Headaches scout the earthquake

like Hives
absorb the swarm's disgrace
He dips in tins, takes down skin and wonders

which furies
send blood where it's needed most?
Rechanneled and re-wired to streets

even when
addicts surround his cities
and purple tracks lasso his Home like draw-strings on

a straitjacket
He remembers He was one of his very own multiples
When cells ran low on blood and spark

they leaped on Him
begged Him shift position
climb up in their stead. No privacy

no publicity yet
Yet, up went rumours

down convictions, no disgrace so fine
as silkworms spinning ass
for spiders that haven't
spun a web in years. Wires unfold

a thousand feet
from tree-top to street-level felonies
and grateful police. The Headache

signals aftershock and addicts cannot
wash off the law deaf as it is
to poverty and addiction to recovery

The Lady Returns

I go to the roof to be with the moon
but the ledge reeks of pigeons and jumpers

I wait for a terrible sentence to begin
as if Heaven's antenna could receive my skinny little fists

I smooth an urgent rush to breathe
finally come my time to sleep but

I wait, air feels different here,
like I am being unmade

I am a brittle flower beaten softly
my family is on the next roof over and

I am the haint that fails to save the final kindness of imitation
by adding one to everything

I sit on a cube of black granite
caught in the pause between flying and fleeing

I charm pillars till earthquakes echo in my jaw
returning me to prior spontaneity where

I drift, not going anywhere,
just a single blessing of opportunity

I am watching Jesus die, to every death an attendant,
a beating god in the heart of the mountain

I am silent words become concern
soundtrack to a blind lip wrapped round a nipple

I am morning mist accosting parkland
turbulence of deep-fried blood nursing burning skin

I sleep in throats of nematodes
fury absorbing the swarm's disgrace

I am under for 22 years and more
to learn the magic of where we begin

I surround secret lakes like rockets
ready to burn our coming to an end

I go to the roof to be with the moon
and settle for shadows instead

I'll be there when you die

After 22 years here's how I know I love you

You should know I woke one Friday morning at 5:07, 23 minutes
before rising for work

22 minutes later I woke again, in tears from a dream of your dying
Young and frightened, your clothes straight out of our everyday

You were dying in a room where I usually work and I checked on you
every few minutes

I got caught with a patient and when I saw you again a colleague
was suctioning phlegm through the catheter he just placed
in your throat

The sound wakes you suddenly, panicked and wide eyed,
and you don't know where you are

You haven't forgotten, you're just too far gone now
but you reach for me and I hold your hand

and I need my colleague to comfort me while I try to calm and comfort you

I missed so much those last few minutes, you went from sick to dying
and I know our time is short and you are still so young

but suddenly so scared and your skin has a sheen I hadn't recognized
but now my own throat tightens

My friend who pierced your throat to help you breathe stays still
to the point of invisibility

and I stroke your forehead hold your hand smell your body changing

I take in the horror of your searching the ceiling for peace or explanation
and then I wake suddenly too, my face wet with tears my chest also heaving

I was tempted to call in sick today
to never leave you again in case this might be true
knowing one day it will be, if our luck continues

And I know I won't be there for every minute to come
but I have to be there when you die

You make me stand here in morning dark, heavy-hearted while you snore
my dream refusing to fade
while I wash and dress for work, calming myself,

not today
not tomorrow

With the end unfolding around us

we need to know how We begin

We would fall asleep, facing each other,
devout like praying children
proud of how we fit together
mirror & universe taking turn
to show each other everything

We would close our eyes to the sounds of
our impending infestation
to the chew of manufacture
and assured co-destruction

We would collapse as if We were posing
slowly moulting into monuments
fertile installations
become fleshy portmanteaux

We would wake as electrified angels
remove our antennae to procreate
build–unbuild one another until
a better behavior is set

It would be as if We were placed here
by an accidental magic

that we might pray like children
to live forever   forever lying still

In the event of an emergency

A warning will sound

Remain calm and follow emergency protocols[1]

Locate nearest emergency kit[††] and secure personal safety before attending to others

Follow radio broadcasts[2,3] for instruction & information on rescue mobilizations

Remain at current location until safety is declared or orders to evacuate are executed[4]

(Remember – Locks, Lights, Out of Sight)

Focus on one goal at a time, identify the most pressing urgency[5]

Remain calm, relax by stretching or listening to music[6]

Practice mindful meditation, document thoughts and utilize guided imagery while waiting[7]

Unleash pets to secure perimeters and search for extra food

Contact neighbours when possible but maintain focus on personal safety[8, 9]

If tumors or infections arise remove as much as tolerable using items from emergency kit[††]

(Bury tissue as far as safe beyond your own perimeter)

Final Protocol (last resort): Abandon Body[10]

[1] Separate protocols apply for local, regional and national threats
[2] Podcasts are not, repeat not, radio broadcasts
[3] Social media will remain unmonitored
[4] If changing locations is unavoidable keep extra-medications on your person at all times
[5] A good place to begin is remaining alive; a better strategy would have been to follow last year's curriculum – Train Adapt Survive. By all means Run and Hide but when all else fails be ready to turn and fight
[6] Bathing is not recommended due to danger of over-exposure
[7] Remove all 'alien waves' from shelters and homes; power down all Siris, Alexas and pods
[8] The forging of new alliances can be a source of reassurance
[9] When all else fails, terminate and dispose
[10] Your brain will try to convince you you're dying. This is a collective delusion predicted in over 90% of simulations and simply represents a reverberation of screams that cannot escape through solid structures. To trigger the Final Protocol, break outer seal and use internal organs to build flotation devices. Use final breaths to inflate your own device and cast off toward escape

---

†† Emergency Kit ††
(these items are bare essentials & should not be considered exhaustive)

Water Food Prescription Medicines First-aid kits and Baby Supplies
Mylar blankets Sleeping-bags Eye-protection and extra clothing
Compass Scissors Work-gloves Flashlights & Batteries
Buckets Towelettes Backpacks & Tube-tents
Matches Candles Light-sticks and knives
Rope Cord Duct-tape & dust-masks
Multi-purpose tools and bleach
Compass Radio Pencil & pad
Chargers Tampons Whistles
Letters of love & farewell
Family documentation
Allergy information
Vaccination record
Blood-group
Can-opener
Bullets
Mask
Cash
TP

Notes

"Qui vincit?" and "//911//9/11//" were inspired by multiple lives touched by opioids, addiction and overdose. My four primary sources of spiritual inspiration were "The Addicts Next Door" by Margaret Talbot (*The New Yorker*, May 29th 2017), *Dreamland: The True Tale of America's Opiate Epidemic* by Sam Quinones (Bloomsbury Press, 2015), *A Town Ruined by Drugs* – a Dark States BBC documentary by Louis Theroux (2017), and the death of my friend Patryk in a foreign country far from his loving wife and son.

"We Are Shine" was inspired by watching *The Shining* three times consecutively and then watching the Vivian Kubrick documentary, *Making the Shining* (Eagle Film SS, 1980), with a focus on the physical and mental abuse experienced by Shelley Duvall on Stanley Kubrick's set.

"L'auteur da fe" was inspired by the Alfred Hitchcock film *Vertigo* (1958), and the announcement that this film which perfectly (unintentionally?) depicts the hierarchical dominion directors hold over female actors is now the 'greatest film of all time' (British Film Institute's Sight and Sound, 2012).

"The Lady Vanishes" is a found poem. The source text appears as "A dream from 1959 Notebook (No. 1)" on page 17 of *Revelations* by Diane Arbus (Random House, 2003).

"Dreams of Deep-River, Ontario" contains lines of dialogue, in italics, from the David Lynch film *Mulholland Drive* (2001). Of interest, Deep-River was a planned community begun in 1944 by the federal government as part of the Manhattan Project to accommodate employees of the nearby Chalk River Nuclear Research Laboratories. Along with Los Alamos, New Mexico and Oak Ridge, Tennessee, Chalk River was an offshoot of the nuclear effort for the allies and scientists, engineers, and tradesmen from around the world who came to work on the Manhattan Project. After World War II, Canada continued with research into the atom and Deep River was situated far enough upwind and upriver of the Chalk River research reactors to theoretically avoid radioactive fallout in the event of an accident. The town was the subject of a Maclean's Magazine article in 1958 by the noted Canadian journalist, editor, and author Peter C. Newman. Entitled, "Deep River: Almost the Perfect Place to Live," the article took a sardonic look at the town as a very odd and isolated place populated by mostly young, male, highly educated and bored scientists and technicians struggling to find things to do with their time: "The Utopian town where our atomic scientists live and play has no crime, no slums, no unemployment and few mothers-in-law." Most David Lynch films & TV series contain references to test detonations of atomic or nuclear devices.

In "Et mu," the first stanza was inspired by a description of the Japanese filmmaker Yasujiro Ozu's grave in *M Train* by Patti Smith (Vintage Canada, 2015). The Greek letter, Mu (μ), is derived from the Egyptian hieroglyphic for water and is used in physiology to denote the class of opioid receptors for which morphine is the prototypical agonist.

"Study of *A Study for the Nurse in Battleship Potemkin*" was inspired by the Francis Bacon painting, "Study for the Nurse in the Film *Battleship Potemkin*" (1957) which was in turn inspired by the famous Odessa steps scene in the film, *Battleship Potemkin* (1925, dir. Sergei Eisenstein).

"Let's all of us agree, protection is the key" was inspired by the film *Double Indemnity* (1944, dir. Billy Wilder) and contains lines of dialogue from the film.

"The Scalded Sea" was inspired by Oliver Sacks' description of the final years of Spalding Gray in his own final book, *Everything In Its Place* (Knopf Canada, 2019, pp 114-128). Further inspiration and perspective was sought in *The Journals of Spalding Gray* (Vintage Books, 2011, ed. Neil Casey).

"Another death in the family" quotes and was inspired by the fearless work of Shelley Winters. This poem is particularly inspired by her work in *A Place in the Sun* (1951, dir. George Stevens) and *Night of the Hunter* (1955, Charles Laughton) where her characters are murdered by men who see her love for them as an obstacle to their true desires. This is true in *A Place in the Sun* whereby her murder frees Montgomery Clift to indulge in one of the most famous onscreen romances (with Elizabeth Taylor) and allows the audience to swoon guilt-free now that his pregnant girlfriend is conveniently 'gone'. This poem also contains a line from The Pixies' song, "I've Been Tired" (C'mon Pilgrim, 4AD Records, 1987).

"On *Elephant* and *Hunger*" was inspired by two films. The first, *Elephant* (1989, dir. Alan Clarke) is a British short depicting sectarian murders that contains no dialogue or recognizable actors. Its title arose from a description of the underlying political and social problems in Northern Ireland in the 1980s as "the elephant in our living room." Its minimalist style is an acknowledged direct influence on Gus Van Sant's 2003 depiction of the Columbine school shootings (also titled *Elephant*). The second, *Hunger*, is a 2008 film directed by Steve McQueen that depicts the hunger strikes and no-wash protests in which Irish republican prisoners held in Belfast's Maze prison struggled to regain the political status as freedom fighters that had been revoked by the British Government in 1976. McQueen received the discovery award at the 33rd Toronto Film Festival and went on to win an Academy Award for directing *12 Years A Slave*.

In "33 RPM" every line is a riff on a (reasonably) well-known album title.

"I will be there" is based on the worst dream I have ever experienced.

"Rebar" was inspired by conditions in Mexico as a drug-based cartel war tore through the country, and conditions in Haiti subsequent to the devastating earthquake of 2010.

"In the event of an emergency" was written three months before the first person tested SARS-CoV-2-positive in North America.

Acknowledgements

The following poems were published (in current or previous iterations) in journals and publications as indicated. My thanks to the editors, readers and publishers who continue to support poetry with those most precious commodities, time spent reading the work of others and time spent thinking on what has been written.

"I am waiting for a terrible sentence to begin" – *580Split; RawArtReview* (Shortlist, 2019 RawArtReview Charles Bukowski Prize)

"Qui Vincit?" – *The Fiddlehead* (Honourable Mention, 2018 Ralph Gustafson Poetry Prize)

"//911//9/11//" "Talisman & Brand" – *Safe Spaces* (Frog Hollow Press, 2017, ed. Shane Neilson)

"We Are Shine" – *longconmagazine*

"Et Mu" – *JAMA*

"Study of A Study for the Nurse in Battleship Potemkin" – *Scrivener Creative Review*; birdburiedpress online

"Another Death in the Family" – *Grain*

"<runprogram#^nightwatch^_creationsim>" – *The Fiddlehead*

"With the end unfolding around us" – *The Movie Lighthouse*, Episode 30; League of Canadian Poets *Poetry & Healing* online, National Poetry Month, April 2020

"In the event of an emergency" – *G U E S T*

Thank You

To Jim Johnstone for shepherding editing and delivering this book to life.

To Denis de Klerck for seeing through the trees and plucking this manuscript from the pile. Thank you to everyone at Mansfield Press for making this dream come true.

To those First Readers into the smoke and flames: Julie Crawford, Robert Colman and DJ Brock, you emerged unscathed with sage advice; gratitude beyond words.

To the Writers: Jim Johnstone, Paul Vermeersch, Dani Couture, David Seymour, Julie Crawford, Robert Colman, David James Brock, Andy Verboom, Annick MacAskill, Jeff Latosik, James Lindsay, Daniel Scott Tysdall, Klara du Plessis, Caitriona Wright, Mark Laliberte, MA|DE, Dom Parisien, Ally Fleming, Alanna Schiffer, Kate Marshall Flaherty, Puneet Dutt, Ian LeTourneau, Anstruther Press, Josh Stewart, Mount Alaska, Shazia, Al Moritz, Jake & Shawna, Kira Shaw, K | F | B, Kramer & Kirby, Ellen Chang-Richardson ... thank you for the community and space within which to painfully grow.

To The Village: Audrey, Cillian & Patrice, Brian & Fiona, Niall & Sara, Aoife & Karen, Todd Binthrax, Adam & Lauren, Arnaud et Marie-Laure, Brendan & Betsy, Catherine & Eric, Chris & Ping, Clyde & Rachelle & Jesse (& Isaac), Emma & Rob, Eric & Tom, Gail & Karen, Galway Ripley & Archer, Gamble & White, Gino & Kelly, Heather Rose, Imelda G & Johnny Mac, Jamie Robertson & Mark Levine, Jammster, Janice lost & found, Jasmine & Julie & Daniel K, Jason & Junebug, Cards Against Humanity, Jim & Erica, John & Jackie, Jon & Mary, Kira & Lawrence, Linda & Scout, Lisa & Jacques, Maha MD, Mary G. & Melissa P., Monica & Chris, David F. & Tara, Mount Alaska, Nate & Joyce, Paul & Bianca, Ellen & Paul, Eli & Rob, Diane & Pete, Pamela Watt (& ICU!), Peter & Amy, Rachel et Aymeric, Renu & Girls, Rob & KMT, Sach & Toon, Sarah & Edouard, SC Brown MD, Stéphanie et Gaëtan, Steve & Pat, The Great Escape, Sandman & Uncle Gregory, Wyndham & Lou, James & Laurie Lighthouse, and you too.

To the Breeders: Patrick Joseph & Patricia Josephine Mc Donnell, Jean-Paul et Josette Jeudy, thank you et merci pour tout. Love to the four of you and to all members of the Mc Donnell, Ward, Jeudy et Moindron clans.

To the Missing: Anthony Mc Donnell, Ann Lovett, Conor Kennedy, Michelle Gilmour, Amanda Haverty, Michael Hughes, Mick Ward & Patryk Winiarski: each time I write I am writing to you.

To the Teacher: Paul Vermeersch, friend mentor teacher cheerleader, one of a handful of men I gladly kiss on the lips (pre-pandemic).

To the Spirit-Guide: Jim Johnstone, all of the above plus one of the few people to whom I accord the word brother. I found the ear, heart and tattooed biceps I never knew I needed so much. Love.

To the End: Audrey, reluctant muse and silent partner you are in so much of this work it would feel like theft not to share it with you. Love of my life, lady of my lake, gentle lips to my febrile forehead, thank you for plucking me from the pile and seeing through the bullshit. cx

Conor Mc Donnell is a physician & poet. He has published two chapbooks, *The Book of Retaliations* (Anstruther Press) and *Safe Spaces* (Frog Hollow Press). He received Honourable Mention for *The Fiddlehead*'s 2018 Ralph Gustafson Poetry Prize, was shortlisted for the *RawArtReview* 2019 Charles Bukowski Prize, and was runner-up in the *Vallum* 2019 Contemporary Poetry Prize. *Recovery Community* is his debut collection, *This Insistent List* is up next …